MIND-BLOWING BASKETBALL FACTS

100 Jaw-Dropping Moments That Changed the Game Forever

FELIX GRAYSON

Copyright © 2025 by MindSpark Publishing

All rights reserved. No part of this book may be reproduced, stored in a retrieval system, or transmitted in any form or by any means—electronic, mechanical, photocopying, recording, or otherwise—without the prior written permission of the publisher, except in the case of brief quotations embodied in critical articles or reviews.

This book is intended to provide general information on the topics discussed and is not intended as a substitute for professional advice. Every effort has been made to ensure accuracy, but the author and publisher assume no responsibility for errors, omissions, or contrary interpretation of the subject matter.

Published by MindSpark Publishing.
Cover design by MindSpark Publishing.

CONTENTS

Before We Dive In... 8

Introduction 10

The Game That Lasted Nearly 6 Hours! 13

Shaq Broke a Backboard... and Nearly Took the Hoop With It! 15

A Free Throw That Took Over an Hour to Count! 17

The Shortest and Tallest Players Once Shared the Same Court! 19

A Game With No Three-Pointers... Despite 29 Attempts! 21

The Game That Ended Before It Even Started! 23

Michael Jordan Was Once Fined for Wearing His Own Sneakers! ... 25

The Only NBA Game With No Jump Ball! 27

The Rookie Finals MVP Who Never Made the Playoffs Again 29

The NBA Player Who Played for Two Teams in One Game! 31

The NBA Game That Stopped... Because of Too Many Free Big Macs! 33

A Player Was Drafted... But Never Actually Existed! 35

Dennis Rodman Once Took a Mid-Season Vacation... to Wrestle! ... 37

The NBA Player Who Never Missed a Game... for 16 Years! 39

The Time an NBA Player Scored for Both Teams! 41

The Player Who Was Traded... for Himself! 43

The NBA Game That Ended in a Forfeit! 45

The NBA Coach Who Was Traded for a Draft Pick! 47

The NBA Game That Was Delayed... by a Bat! 49

The Player Who Scored 100 Points Before Wilt! 51

The Time an NBA Game Was Played Outside... and It Went Wrong! 53

The NBA Player Who Played for 12 Teams… in 12 Seasons! 55

The NBA Player Who Changed His Name to Promote His Shoes! 57

The NBA Game That Had Three Halftimes! 59

The Player Who Was Drafted… but Never Played Basketball! 61

The NBA Team That Drafted the Wrong Player… by Mistake! 63

The NBA Game That Was Delayed by a Slippery Floor! 65

The NBA Player Who Got Ejected Before the Game Started! 67

The NBA Game That Was Delayed… By a Broken Toilet! 69

The Player Who Wore Five Different Jersey Numbers in One Season! 71

The NBA Player Who Got Traded… While Playing a Game! 73

The NBA Player Who Scored… But Had His Points Erased! 75

The NBA Game That Featured Only Four Players! 77

The NBA Game That Was Delayed… Because the Court Was Too Short! ... 79

The NBA Player Who Scored a Basket… in the Wrong Hoop! 81

The NBA Team That Once Had Zero Points After a Quarter! 83

The NBA Game That Was Delayed… Because of Too Much Fog! 85

The NBA Player Who Played the Most Minutes… Without Ever Scoring! .. 87

The Only Finals MVP Who Never Started a Game! 89

The Time an NBA Player Tried to Score… on the Wrong Basket! 91

The Player Who Signed a $90M Shoe Deal Before His First Game! 93

The NBA Game That Ended in a Tie After Teams Ran Out of Players 95

The NBA Player Who Was Traded… for a Copy Machine! 97

The NBA Player Who Made the League… Without Being Drafted! 99

The NBA Game That Was Delayed… by a Gatorade Explosion! 101

The NBA Player Who Scored 70 Points… and Lost the Game! 103

The NBA Game That Was Delayed… Because of a Stuck Zamboni! 105

The NBA Player Who Was Fined… for Kissing a Referee! 107

The NBA Player Who Played for the Same Team… Twice in One Game! .. 109

The NBA Game That Was Delayed… by a Snake in the Locker Room! 111

The NBA Player Suspended… for Bringing Popcorn to Practice 113

The NBA Player Who Was Ejected… for Air-Guitar Celebration! 115

The Player Who Wore Two Different Jersey Numbers in One Game 117

The NBA Game That Was Delayed… Because the Basket Was Too Tall! ... 119

The NBA Player Who Missed a Game… Because of a Peanut Allergy! 121

The NBA Player Who Got Ejected… for Dancing! 123

The NBA Game That Was Delayed… Because of a Broken Shot Clock! 125

The Player Who Signed a $30M Deal… Then Retired the Same Day 127

The NBA Game That Was Delayed… Because of a Free Taco Promotion! . 129

The NBA Player Who Once Scored 0 Points… But Still Won Finals MVP! 131

The NBA Game That Was Delayed… Because of a Missing Referee! 133

The NBA Player Who Was Drafted… But Didn't Exist! 135

The NBA Player Who Got a Technical Foul… for High-Fiving a Referee! . 137

The NBA Player Who Lost a Shoe… and Kept Playing! 139

The Player Who Wore Goggles After a Brutal Eye Injury 141

The NBA Game That Was Delayed… Because of a Fire Alarm! 143

The NBA Player Who Once Got a Triple-Double… Without Points! 145

The NBA Player Who Played in 5 Different Decades! 147

The NBA Game That Was Delayed… Because of a Missing Net! 149

The NBA Player Who Picked Fast Food Over Basketball 151

The NBA Player Who Scored 13 Points in 33 Seconds! 153

The NBA Game That Was Played in Total Silence! 155

The NBA Player Who Once Scored 100 Points… in Just 20 Minutes! 157

The NBA Player Who Was Ejected… for Yawning! 159

The NBA Game That Was Delayed… Because of a Leaking Roof! 161

The NBA Player Who Signed a Contract… That Paid Him for 30 Years! ... 163

The NBA Game That Was Delayed… Because of Too Much Popcorn! 165

The NBA Player Who Played a Game Wearing a Hospital Wristband 167

The NBA Player Who Was Traded… for a Washing Machine! 169

The NBA Player Who Once Blocked 17 Shots in a Single Game! 171

The NBA Game That Was Delayed… Because of a Broken Backboard! 173

The NBA Player Who Once Recorded a "Double Triple-Double"! 175

The NBA Game That Was Played on a Court With No Three-Point Line! . 177

The NBA Player Who Wore the Wrong Shorts… for an Entire Game! 179

The NBA Player Who Was Fined… for Wearing Too Many Headbands! .. 181

The NBA Player Who Scored a Basket… While Lying on the Floor! 183

The NBA Game Delayed by a Broken Shot Clock 185

The Player Who Scored 50 Points… Without a Single Three 187

The NBA Player Who Wore Three Different Jerseys in One Game! 189

The Player Who Signed a Contract… Then Retired the Same Day 191

The NBA Game That Was Delayed… Because the Lights Went Out! 193

The NBA Player Who Scored 0 Points… But Still Had a Perfect Game! 195

The NBA Game Delayed by a Player Hanging on the Rim 197

The Player Who Blocked More Shots Than an Entire Team 199

The NBA Player Who Got Ejected… Before the Game Even Started! 201

The NBA Game That Was Delayed… Because a Bat Invaded the Court! ... 203

The NBA Player Who Once Played for Two Teams… in the Same Game! . 205

The Only Finals MVP Who Never Started a Game 207

The NBA Player Who Was Drafted… But Never Played a Single Game! ... 209

The NBA Player Who Scored 100 Points... But There's No Video Proof! .. 211

Conclusion 212

Acknowledgements 214

About the Author 216

BEFORE WE DIVE IN...

Did you know that this is just **one** of many **mind-blowing** books waiting to be discovered?

What if I told you there's a **world of jaw-dropping, unbelievable, and downright bizarre facts** across **sports, science, history, mysteries, and more**—each one packed with stories that will **challenge what you thought you knew?**

EVER WONDERED WHAT IT'S LIKE TO...

- Witness **record-breaking Olympic moments** that defy human limits?

- Explore **real-life conspiracy theories** that sound too wild to be true?

- Discover **unsolved mysteries** that still leave experts baffled?

- Learn about **billionaires, stock market crashes, and money secrets?**

- Find out how **robots, AI, and space travel** are shaping the future?

- Experience the **most extreme sports, legendary battles, and shocking events?**

This is just the beginning. The **100 Mind-Blowing series** covers it **all.**

WANT TO SEE WHAT'S NEXT?

Go to **FelixGrayson.com** and explore the **growing collection** of books and audiobooks that will **entertain, amaze, and keep you coming back for more.**

Curiosity doesn't stop here—this is just the beginning. What will blow your mind next?

INTRODUCTION

Welcome to *100 Mind-Blowing Basketball Facts*, a collection designed to make you say, **"No way... that actually happened?"** From unbelievable records to bizarre rule changes, from legendary performances to pure chaos on the court, this book is packed with **stories that will change the way you see the game.**

Have you ever heard about the NBA player who played for **two different teams in the same game**? Or the time a game was **delayed because of a bat invasion**? What about the player who **scored 50 points without taking a single three-pointer**? These are just a few of the jaw-dropping moments waiting for you inside. Each fact has been carefully selected to **surprise, entertain, and leave you in awe of basketball's wildest moments.**

Whether you're a **die-hard fan**, a **casual hoops watcher**, or just someone looking for **some epic conversation starters**, this book has **something for you**. Read it from start to finish or flip to a random page and let fate decide your next mind-blowing fact. **There's no wrong way to experience this ride through basketball history!**

So grab a seat, maybe even a basketball, and get ready to **dive into the most insane, unexpected, and legendary moments in hoops history.** By the end, you might just have a few new favorite stories to share—and some new trivia skills to impress your friends!

Let's tip this off!

Mind-Blowing Basketball Fact #1

MIND-BLOWING BASKETBALL FACT #1

THE GAME THAT LASTED NEARLY 6 HOURS!

The longest game in NBA history took place on January 6, 1951, between the Indianapolis Olympians and the Rochester Royals. The game went into **a record-setting six overtimes**, lasting an astonishing **78 minutes of playtime**. Despite the marathon battle, the final score was shockingly low—**Indianapolis won 75-73**, proving that endurance, not just skill, was the key to victory that night!

Mind-Blowing Basketball Fact #2

MIND-BLOWING BASKETBALL FACT #2

SHAQ BROKE A BACKBOARD... AND NEARLY TOOK THE HOOP WITH IT!

On April 23, 1993, during a game against the New Jersey Nets, **Shaquille O'Neal** unleashed a monster dunk that completely shattered the backboard! But that wasn't the craziest part—the force of his slam **broke the entire support structure, causing the hoop to collapse** onto the court.

Shaq's sheer power led the NBA to **reinforce all backboards and rims** to withstand future dunks from dominant big men. From that moment on, the league knew: **Shaq wasn't just breaking records—he was breaking equipment too!**

Mind-Blowing Basketball Fact #3

MIND-BLOWING BASKETBALL FACT #3

A FREE THROW THAT TOOK OVER AN HOUR TO COUNT!

In a bizarre turn of events, an **NBA free throw once took more than an hour to count!** During a 1961 game between the Chicago Packers and the St. Louis Hawks, future Hall of Famer **Bob Pettit** stepped to the line for a routine free throw.

But right as he released the shot, the arena **suffered a power outage**, plunging the court into darkness! The officials had to **pause the game for over an hour** until the lights were restored. When play finally resumed, they counted Pettit's free throw—meaning it had been **stuck in limbo for an entire hour** before officially going on the scoreboard!

Basketball may be fast-paced, but sometimes, even a **single point** can take forever to land!

Mind-Blowing Basketball Fact #4

MIND-BLOWING BASKETBALL FACT #4

THE SHORTEST AND TALLEST PLAYERS ONCE SHARED THE SAME COURT!

In one of the most iconic moments in NBA history, **the tallest and shortest players ever faced off in the same game!**

On March 6, 1987, the **7-foot-7 giant Manute Bol** and the **5-foot-3 speedster Muggsy Bogues** played together as teammates for the Washington Bullets during a preseason game. With a staggering **28-inch height difference**, the duo looked like something out of a basketball cartoon!

Despite their extreme size contrast, both players had impressive careers—Manute **dominated with shot-blocking**, while Muggsy **became one of the fastest, most tenacious defenders in NBA history.**

A true reminder that in basketball, **size matters... but heart and skill matter even more!**

Mind-Blowing Basketball Fact #5

MIND-BLOWING BASKETBALL FACT #5

A GAME WITH NO THREE-POINTERS... DESPITE 29 ATTEMPTS!

On February 16, 1990, the **Denver Nuggets** faced off against the **Portland Trail Blazers** in what became one of the most **historically bizarre shooting performances** in NBA history.

Denver attempted a jaw-dropping **29 three-pointers** throughout the game... and **missed every single one!** That's right—**0-for-29 from deep!**

To this day, this remains the most **three-point attempts without a single make** in an NBA game. A reminder that even in the world's greatest league, **some nights, the basket just won't cooperate!**

Mind-Blowing Basketball Fact #6

MIND-BLOWING BASKETBALL FACT #6

THE GAME THAT ENDED BEFORE IT EVEN STARTED!

On December 14, 1977, a scheduled game between the **Los Angeles Lakers and the Milwaukee Bucks** was set to take place at the Forum in LA. Fans packed the arena, players warmed up, and the referees were ready.

But there was **one big problem—the Lakers forgot to bring their jerseys!**

Due to a bizarre logistical mishap, the Lakers' uniforms were left behind, and they had no back-ups available. With no way to distinguish teams on the court, **the NBA was forced to postpone the game before the opening tip-off!**

It remains one of the only times in league history that a game was **canceled before a single second was played**—all because of a forgotten bag!

Mind-Blowing Basketball Fact #7

MIND-BLOWING BASKETBALL FACT #7

MICHAEL JORDAN WAS ONCE FINED FOR WEARING HIS OWN SNEAKERS!

Michael Jordan's signature sneakers are some of the most legendary shoes in history, but did you know that **the NBA once banned them?**

In 1984, when Jordan debuted the original **Air Jordan 1s**, the league ruled that they **violated uniform policy** due to their bold red-and-black color scheme. The NBA fined Jordan **$5,000 every time he wore them in a game!**

Nike saw this as the ultimate marketing opportunity and **gladly paid every fine** on Jordan's behalf. The controversy turned the Air Jordans into a global sensation, **forever changing sneaker culture and basketball fashion.**

Mind-Blowing Basketball Fact #8

MIND-BLOWING BASKETBALL FACT #8

THE ONLY NBA GAME WITH NO JUMP BALL!

A basketball game always starts with a **jump ball at center court**—except for one bizarre exception!

On November 7, 1978, the **Philadelphia 76ers** and the **New Jersey Nets** tipped off their game as usual... but just minutes in, a **brawl erupted between players.** The fight escalated so quickly that the referees had no choice but to **call off the game and reschedule it for a later date.**

When the teams met again to replay the game, the NBA made a strange ruling: since the original game had technically started, **they would resume play from where they left off—without a new jump ball!**

To this day, it remains **the only NBA game in history to begin without a tip-off!**

Mind-Blowing Basketball Fact #9

MIND-BLOWING BASKETBALL FACT #9

THE ROOKIE FINALS MVP WHO NEVER MADE THE PLAYOFFS AGAIN

Winning **NBA Finals MVP** is the ultimate honor, but only one player ever won it as a rookie—**and never made the playoffs again!**

In 1980, **Magic Johnson** stepped up in the NBA Finals after Kareem Abdul-Jabbar got injured. In **Game 6**, Magic, just 20 years old, played **all five positions**, dropped **42 points, 15 rebounds, and 7 assists**, and led the Lakers to the championship. He became the **only rookie in history to win Finals MVP!**

On the other hand, **Andre Iguodala** holds the strangest stat in Finals MVP history—**after winning the award in 2015, he never played in another playoff game for the rest of his career.**

Two players, two opposite fates—but both forever part of NBA history!

Mind-Blowing Basketball Fact #10

MIND-BLOWING BASKETBALL FACT #10

THE NBA PLAYER WHO PLAYED FOR TWO TEAMS IN ONE GAME!

It sounds impossible, but **one player actually played for both teams in a single NBA game!**

On November 8, 1978, **Kansas City Kings' forward Ralph Simpson** was traded to the **Denver Nuggets** in the middle of a game. Because of the unique timing of the trade, Simpson **switched jerseys at halftime** and finished the second half playing for his new team!

This bizarre situation was only possible due to **looser trade rules in the 1970s**, making it a one-of-a-kind moment in NBA history. Today, strict player clearance procedures **make it impossible for a player to ever pull off this feat again!**

Mind-Blowing Basketball Fact #11

MIND-BLOWING BASKETBALL FACT #11

THE NBA GAME THAT STOPPED... BECAUSE OF TOO MANY FREE BIG MACS!

NBA teams often run fun promotions, but one night, a free burger giveaway **completely disrupted a game!**

The **Chicago Bulls** had a long-standing deal: if the team scored **100 points or more** at home, every fan in attendance **won a free Big Mac from McDonald's.**

On March 21, 2007, with the Bulls sitting at **98 points** in the final seconds against the Denver Nuggets, the crowd went **wild**, chanting for one more bucket. The players responded—by launching **three-pointers and half-court shots**, completely ignoring normal play!

When **Andres Nocioni** finally scored to hit 100, the United Center **erupted in celebration**, delaying the game as fans **cheered more for their free burgers than the actual win!**

Mind-Blowing Basketball Fact #12

MIND-BLOWING BASKETBALL FACT #12

A PLAYER WAS DRAFTED... BUT NEVER ACTUALLY EXISTED!

In one of the strangest pranks in sports history, a **completely fictional player** was selected in the 1977 NBA Draft!

A group of **Milwaukee Bucks** front office staff, looking to have some fun, submitted the name **"John Smith" from "Sensebaugh State"** as a draft pick. The problem? **Neither the player nor the school actually existed!**

The NBA quickly realized the joke and **voided the selection**, but the incident remains a hilarious reminder that even professional sports can have their share of pranks.

Mind-Blowing Basketball Fact #13

DENNIS RODMAN ONCE TOOK A MID-SEASON VACATION... TO WRESTLE!

Dennis Rodman was known for his wild personality, but in 1998, he pulled off **one of the most insane mid-season stunts in NBA history—he left the Chicago Bulls during the NBA Finals to join a wrestling match!**

Right in the middle of the championship series against the Utah Jazz, Rodman **skipped a team practice** to appear on **WCW Monday Nitro** alongside Hulk Hogan. He even got into a scripted brawl with Karl Malone—**the same player he was battling in the Finals!**

Despite the chaos, Rodman returned and helped the Bulls **win their sixth championship**, proving that he could dominate on the court... and in the wrestling ring!

Mind-Blowing Basketball Fact #14

MIND-BLOWING BASKETBALL FACT #14

THE NBA PLAYER WHO NEVER MISSED A GAME... FOR 16 YEARS!

Imagine playing **every single game** for over a decade—without ever sitting out! That's exactly what **A.C. Green** did, earning him the legendary nickname: **"The Iron Man" of the NBA.**

From **November 19, 1986, to April 18, 2001**, Green played an **unbelievable 1,192 consecutive games**—the longest streak in NBA history. He endured **injuries, trades, and even tooth extractions**, but he never let anything keep him off the court.

To put it into perspective, Green played **16 straight seasons without missing a single game**, a record that is almost impossible to break in today's era of load management!

Mind-Blowing Basketball Fact #15

MIND-BLOWING BASKETBALL FACT #15

THE TIME AN NBA PLAYER SCORED FOR BOTH TEAMS!

Scoring points in an NBA game is normal—but what if you accidentally scored for the **wrong team?**

That's exactly what happened to **Ricky Davis** on January 30, 2003. While playing for the Cleveland Cavaliers, Davis **accidentally tipped the ball into his own basket**, giving the **Utah Jazz two free points!**

The funniest part? The Jazz **credited the points to their nearest player**, making it seem like he had scored without even touching the ball!

This wasn't the first time it happened in NBA history, but it remains one of the most hilarious and bizarre self-inflicted blunders ever caught on camera.

Mind-Blowing Basketball Fact #16

MIND-BLOWING BASKETBALL FACT #16

THE PLAYER WHO WAS TRADED... FOR HIMSELF!

NBA trades can get complicated, but in one of the strangest transactions ever, a player was actually **traded for himself!**

In 1994, the **Cleveland Cavaliers** traded **point guard Muggsy Bogues** to the **Washington Bullets** in exchange for another player and a **future draft pick.** However, a few months later, the Cavs and Bullets **reworked the deal**—and part of the compensation package ended up being... **Muggsy Bogues himself!**

That means he was **technically traded for his own contract**, making it one of the most bizarre trades in league history.

Mind-Blowing Basketball Fact #17

MIND-BLOWING BASKETBALL FACT #17

THE NBA GAME THAT ENDED IN A FORFEIT!

NBA teams fight hard to win, but one team lost **without even finishing the game!**

On **November 19, 2004**, the infamous **"Malice at the Palace"** brawl broke out between the **Indiana Pacers and Detroit Pistons**. After a heated scuffle on the court, a fan **threw a drink at Ron Artest**, causing an all-out melee between **players and fans.**

With chaos erupting in the stands, the referees **had no choice but to call off the game**. The result? The **Pacers were officially awarded the win** because the Pistons were ruled unable to continue.

It remains one of the only **forfeited games in modern NBA history**—and the most shocking fight the league has ever seen!

Mind-Blowing Basketball Fact #18

MIND-BLOWING BASKETBALL FACT #18

THE NBA COACH WHO WAS TRADED FOR A DRAFT PICK!

Players get traded all the time—but did you know that **an NBA coach was once traded for a draft pick?**

In 2000, the **Boston Celtics** wanted to hire **Doc Rivers** as their head coach, but he was still under contract with the **Orlando Magic**. Instead of waiting for his deal to expire, the Celtics did something unheard of—**they traded a first-round draft pick to Orlando in exchange for his coaching rights!**

That's right—Doc Rivers became one of the only coaches in history to be **traded like a player!** The move paid off, as he later led the Celtics to an **NBA Championship in 2008.**

Mind-Blowing Basketball Fact #19

MIND-BLOWING BASKETBALL FACT #19

THE NBA GAME THAT WAS DELAYED... BY A BAT!

NBA games have been delayed for many reasons, but **one time, an actual bat took over the court!**

On **October 31, 2009 (fittingly, Halloween night),** a game between the **San Antonio Spurs and Sacramento Kings** came to a sudden halt when a **real bat** swooped down into the arena, flying around the players!

As the crowd gasped and security scrambled, **Spurs legend Manu Ginóbili took matters into his own hands**—literally. He **swatted the bat out of mid-air with his bare hand**, instantly becoming a viral sensation.

The bat was safely removed, the game resumed, and Ginóbili walked away as the only NBA player with **both a championship ring and a bat-hunting highlight!**

Mind-Blowing Basketball Fact #20

THE PLAYER WHO SCORED 100 POINTS BEFORE WILT!

Wilt Chamberlain's legendary **100-point game** in 1962 is the most famous scoring feat in basketball history—but did you know another player **hit the 100-point mark first?**

Back in **1953**, a little-known player named **Bevo Francis** scored an **unreal 116 points in a single college game** while playing for Rio Grande College. His performance was so shocking that some didn't believe it was real!

While his record didn't happen in the NBA, it paved the way for future high-scoring performances, proving that a **triple-digit game was possible**—nearly a decade before Wilt made history!

Mind-Blowing Basketball Fact #21

MIND-BLOWING BASKETBALL FACT #21

THE TIME AN NBA GAME WAS PLAYED OUTSIDE... AND IT WENT WRONG!

In 2008, the NBA decided to do something unique—**host a preseason game outdoors** for the first time in modern history. The matchup featured the **Phoenix Suns and the Denver Nuggets** at the **Indian Wells Tennis Garden in California.**

But there was one major problem—**the weather!**

Players struggled with **wind gusts, a slippery court from humidity, and unusual sightlines due to the open sky.** Shooting percentages **plummeted**, and the game became a defensive grind rather than an entertaining showcase.

After the sloppy 77-72 Suns win, the NBA **never attempted an outdoor game again,** proving that basketball is best played **inside the arena!**

Mind-Blowing Basketball Fact #22

MIND-BLOWING BASKETBALL FACT #22

THE NBA PLAYER WHO PLAYED FOR 12 TEAMS... IN 12 SEASONS!

Most players spend their careers with just a few teams, but **one NBA journeyman took team-hopping to the extreme!**

Jim Jackson, a talented shooting guard, played for **12 different teams in 12 seasons**, setting a record for the most teams played for in the shortest amount of time.

His career included stints with the **Mavericks, Nets, 76ers, Warriors, Trail Blazers, Hawks, Cavaliers, Heat, Kings, Rockets, Suns, and Lakers!**

Despite constantly changing jerseys, Jackson remained a solid contributor, proving that **no matter where he played, he could always make an impact.**

Mind-Blowing Basketball Fact #23

MIND-BLOWING BASKETBALL FACT #23

THE NBA PLAYER WHO CHANGED HIS NAME TO PROMOTE HIS SHOES!

Athletes often sign shoe deals, but **one NBA player took it to the next level—by legally changing his name to advertise his sneakers!**

In 2011, **Ron Artest** shocked the world by officially changing his name to **Metta World Peace**. While he claimed it was to promote positivity, insiders speculated that the move was also part of a **brilliant marketing strategy** for his new sneaker brand, the "Ball'n" shoe line.

The name change grabbed massive media attention, putting both **him and his shoes in the spotlight.** Whether it was for business or personal growth, one thing is for sure—**no one forgot the name Metta World Peace!**

Mind-Blowing Basketball Fact #24

MIND-BLOWING BASKETBALL FACT #24

THE NBA GAME THAT HAD THREE HALFTIMES!

Every basketball game has **two halves**—but one bizarre NBA game actually had **three halftimes!**

On **November 9, 1983**, the **San Diego Clippers** (now the LA Clippers) faced the **Houston Rockets** in a game that was **unexpectedly stopped after halftime due to a power outage.**

The game was **rescheduled and restarted weeks later**, but because the league ruled that the first half still counted, the teams **had to play another halftime!**

This meant the players experienced **two separate halftimes in the same game—once on the original night and again during the replay.** It remains one of the weirdest scheduling mishaps in NBA history!

Mind-Blowing Basketball Fact #25

MIND-BLOWING BASKETBALL FACT #25

THE PLAYER WHO WAS DRAFTED... BUT NEVER PLAYED BASKETBALL!

Getting drafted into the NBA usually means years of training, but one player **was selected without ever playing an actual basketball game!**

In the **1977 NBA Draft,** the **New Orleans Jazz** picked **Lusia Harris**—the first and only woman ever officially drafted by an NBA team. Harris was a dominant **college basketball star**, but because the NBA was a men's league, she **never played in an official NBA game.**

Even crazier, in 1969, the **San Francisco Warriors** drafted a player named **Denis Pétrovic**—who turned out to be a **completely fictional person!**

These wild draft-day moments prove that **even the NBA isn't immune to surprises!**

Mind-Blowing Basketball Fact #26

MIND-BLOWING BASKETBALL FACT #26

THE NBA TEAM THAT DRAFTED THE WRONG PLAYER... BY MISTAKE!

The NBA Draft is a high-stakes event, but in 1986, one team made **one of the most embarrassing mistakes ever.**

The **Chicago Bulls** were set to select **North Carolina star Brad Sellers** with their first-round pick. But when the front office called in their selection, a **miscommunication occurred**, and the NBA mistakenly announced a different name!

For a few minutes, the Bulls had **drafted the wrong player**, causing chaos in their war room. Fortunately, they **quickly corrected the mistake**, and Sellers became their official pick.

This near-disaster proved that even in the NBA, **one small slip-up can change everything!**

Mind-Blowing Basketball Fact #27

MIND-BLOWING BASKETBALL FACT #27

THE NBA GAME THAT WAS DELAYED BY A SLIPPERY FLOOR!

NBA games have been postponed for many reasons, but one game was nearly **canceled mid-play**—because the court was **too slippery to run on!**

On **December 8, 2016,** the **Sacramento Kings** were set to play the **Philadelphia 76ers** when players noticed **they couldn't keep their footing.** The culprit? A **rare weather phenomenon** caused excessive moisture inside the arena, making the hardwood **as slick as ice.**

Despite multiple attempts to dry the floor, the conditions remained **dangerous**, and after nearly an hour of delays, the NBA **called off the game entirely!**

It's one of the few times in history that **Mother Nature literally stopped an NBA game!**

Mind-Blowing Basketball Fact #28

MIND-BLOWING BASKETBALL FACT #28

THE NBA PLAYER WHO GOT EJECTED BEFORE THE GAME STARTED!

Getting ejected from an NBA game is rare, but one player was thrown out before the opening tip-off!

On **December 3, 2019, New York Knicks forward Marcus Morris** got into a heated argument with the referees **during pregame warmups.** The officials didn't like his attitude, and before he could even step on the court for a single second of play, **they ejected him from the game!**

This made him one of the **only players in NBA history to be disqualified before the game even officially began**—a record that's as bizarre as it is unforgettable!

Mind-Blowing Basketball Fact #29

MIND-BLOWING BASKETBALL FACT #29

THE NBA GAME THAT WAS DELAYED... BY A BROKEN TOILET!

NBA games have been delayed for all sorts of reasons, but in **1993**, a game was put on hold for one of the strangest yet—a **toilet malfunction!**

During a matchup between the **Golden State Warriors and San Antonio Spurs,** a major plumbing issue at the Oakland Coliseum Arena **caused a flood in the team's locker rooms.** Water leaked onto the court, and maintenance crews scrambled to fix the problem.

The game was **delayed for over an hour** while workers dealt with the unexpected bathroom disaster. Eventually, play resumed, but fans never forgot the night when an **NBA game was nearly flushed away!**

Mind-Blowing Basketball Fact #30

MIND-BLOWING BASKETBALL FACT #30

THE PLAYER WHO WORE FIVE DIFFERENT JERSEY NUMBERS IN ONE SEASON!

Most NBA players stick with one jersey number, but **one player changed his number so many times, fans could barely keep up!**

During the **2004-05 season, Orlando Magic guard Mike James** set a bizarre record by wearing **five different jersey numbers** in a single season. Due to **trades, roster changes, and uniform availability issues**, James played games wearing #13, #7, #8, #1, and #5!

To this day, he holds the record for **the most jersey number changes in one season**, making it nearly impossible for fans to buy the "right" Mike James jersey at the time!

Mind-Blowing Basketball Fact #31

MIND-BLOWING BASKETBALL FACT #31

THE NBA PLAYER WHO GOT TRADED… WHILE PLAYING A GAME!

NBA players know trades can happen anytime, but **one player found out he was traded… in the middle of a game!**

On **February 6, 2019, Harrison Barnes** was playing for the **Dallas Mavericks** against the **Charlotte Hornets** when news broke that he had been **traded to the Sacramento Kings—while he was still on the court!**

Midway through the fourth quarter, Barnes was **subbed out and left on the bench**, unaware that social media was already buzzing with the trade announcement. By the time he found out, he was already a Sacramento King!

It was a surreal reminder that in the NBA, **you can go from one team to another in the blink of an eye!**

Mind-Blowing Basketball Fact #32

THE NBA PLAYER WHO SCORED... BUT HAD HIS POINTS ERASED!

Scoring in the NBA is supposed to be permanent, but one player **had his points completely erased from the record books!**

On **March 8, 1969, Chicago Bulls guard Bob Boozer** played in a game against the **Phoenix Suns** and put up **a solid 21-point performance.** However, due to a **scoring error,** the game was **ordered to be replayed from the start weeks later!**

When the teams met again for the do-over, Boozer struggled and only scored **14 points,** meaning he **lost seven points from his career total**—making him one of the only players in history to have official NBA points vanish!

A tough break, but proof that in basketball, **even the scoreboard isn't always final!**

Mind-Blowing Basketball Fact #33

THE NBA GAME THAT FEATURED ONLY FOUR PLAYERS!

An NBA team needs **five players on the court**, but in one historic game, a team was forced to finish with just **four!**

On **January 8, 2010**, the **Golden State Warriors** faced the **Milwaukee Bucks** with a heavily depleted roster due to injuries. By the fourth quarter, **foul trouble forced them to play with only four players on the floor!**

Despite being outnumbered, the Warriors fought until the final buzzer, creating one of the most **unbelievable shorthanded performances in NBA history.**

This rare moment showed that in basketball, **sometimes, the biggest fight comes from the smallest squad!**

Mind-Blowing Basketball Fact #34

MIND-BLOWING BASKETBALL FACT #34

THE NBA GAME THAT WAS DELAYED... BECAUSE THE COURT WAS TOO SHORT!

NBA courts are **always regulation size**, but in 1994, one game was delayed because the **floor was accidentally built too short!**

Before a **Chicago Bulls vs. Milwaukee Bucks** preseason game in **La Crosse, Wisconsin,** officials discovered that the court **wasn't the standard 94 feet long**—it was **about a foot too short!**

With no quick fix available, the game was **delayed as workers frantically tried to adjust the floor.** Eventually, the game proceeded on the slightly smaller court, making it one of the weirdest venue mishaps in NBA history!

A true reminder that in basketball, **every inch counts!**

Mind-Blowing Basketball Fact #35

MIND-BLOWING BASKETBALL FACT #35

THE NBA PLAYER WHO SCORED A BASKET... IN THE WRONG HOOP!

Scoring is every player's goal, but one NBA star accidentally **put points on the board for the wrong team!**

During a game in **1977, Cleveland Cavaliers forward Bobby Wilson** grabbed a rebound and, in the chaos, **instinctively put the ball back up for an easy layup.** The problem? **He shot on the wrong basket!**

Wilson's accidental bucket **gave two free points to the opposing team**, and to make things worse, those points ended up **deciding the game.** His mistake is now one of the most unforgettable blunders in NBA history!

A lesson to always **check which hoop you're aiming for!**

Mind-Blowing Basketball Fact #36

MIND-BLOWING BASKETBALL FACT #36

THE NBA TEAM THAT ONCE HAD ZERO POINTS AFTER A QUARTER!

Scoring in the NBA is never easy, but one team **set the ultimate record for futility**—by failing to score a **single point in an entire quarter!**

On **November 27, 1950,** the **Fort Wayne Pistons** (now the Detroit Pistons) faced the **Minneapolis Lakers** in one of the slowest games ever played. The Pistons struggled so badly that they **finished the fourth quarter with ZERO points!**

Their final score? A painful **18 total points**, making it the **lowest-scoring game in NBA history** (they still won, 19-18).

A reminder that **sometimes, defense really does win games!**

Mind-Blowing Basketball Fact #37

MIND-BLOWING BASKETBALL FACT #37

THE NBA GAME THAT WAS DELAYED... BECAUSE OF TOO MUCH FOG!

Indoor basketball games are usually safe from the weather, but one NBA matchup had to be delayed due to **thick fog—inside the arena!**

On **December 9, 1990,** the **San Antonio Spurs** were playing the **Minnesota Timberwolves** in the **Alamodome**, a massive multi-purpose stadium. Because of poor air circulation, **heat from the court mixed with the cold air from the arena's ice rink**, creating a **heavy fog that covered the entire court!**

Players and referees **struggled to see** through the haze, forcing the game to be **delayed until the fog cleared.**

A truly rare moment where **Mother Nature found a way to mess with an indoor sport!**

Mind-Blowing Basketball Fact #38

MIND-BLOWING BASKETBALL FACT #38

THE NBA PLAYER WHO PLAYED THE MOST MINUTES... WITHOUT EVER SCORING!

Most NBA players dream of scoring points, but one player **set a bizarre record—by playing the most minutes without ever making a basket!**

Joel Anthony, a defensive specialist, played **2,924 career minutes** over multiple seasons before finally scoring his first NBA field goal. Despite his offensive struggles, Anthony remained a valuable role player, focusing on **shot-blocking and defense** rather than scoring.

His record proves that in basketball, **you don't always need to score to make an impact!**

Mind-Blowing Basketball Fact #39

MIND-BLOWING BASKETBALL FACT #39

THE ONLY FINALS MVP WHO NEVER STARTED A GAME!

Winning **NBA Finals MVP** is an elite honor, but one player made history by winning it **without ever starting a game!**

In **2015, Andre Iguodala** of the Golden State Warriors came off the bench for most of the season, but when the **NBA Finals** arrived, everything changed. Midway through the series, coach **Steve Kerr inserted him into the starting lineup** to slow down LeBron James. The move worked—**Iguodala played lockdown defense and hit clutch shots**, helping the Warriors win the title.

Despite not being a regular starter, Iguodala was named **Finals MVP**, becoming the **first and only player in NBA history to win the award without starting every game of the series!**

Mind-Blowing Basketball Fact #40

MIND-BLOWING BASKETBALL FACT #40

THE TIME AN NBA PLAYER TRIED TO SCORE... ON THE WRONG BASKET!

NBA players love chasing stats, but one player took it **way too far**—by trying to **intentionally score on his own basket!**

On **March 16, 2003, Cleveland Cavaliers guard Ricky Davis** had **26 points, 12 assists, and 9 rebounds** late in the game. Desperate for a triple-double, he **took an uncontested shot at his own basket, hoping to grab the "rebound" to get his 10th board!**

The opposing team and referees **immediately called him out**, and Davis was **fouled hard by a furious Utah Jazz player.** The league **refused to count the stunt as a legitimate rebound,** and Davis became infamous for one of the most shameless stat-padding attempts in NBA history!

Mind-Blowing Basketball Fact #41

MIND-BLOWING BASKETBALL FACT #41

THE PLAYER WHO SIGNED A $90M SHOE DEAL BEFORE HIS FIRST GAME!

Most NBA players need to prove themselves before landing massive endorsements, but **one rookie secured a $90 million sneaker deal before ever stepping on the court!**

In **2003, LeBron James** entered the NBA as one of the most hyped prospects ever. Before playing a single game, he signed a **seven-year, $90 million contract with Nike**, the biggest shoe deal ever given to a rookie at the time.

The gamble paid off—LeBron became an all-time great, and his signature sneakers **generated billions in revenue**, making him one of the most successful athletes in sports marketing history.

A true example of **betting on potential... and winning big!**

Mind-Blowing Basketball Fact #42

MIND-BLOWING BASKETBALL FACT #42

THE NBA GAME THAT ENDED IN A TIE AFTER TEAMS RAN OUT OF PLAYERS

NBA games **never** end in ties—except for one unbelievable matchup where both teams literally **ran out of players!**

On **November 9, 1949,** the **Anderson Packers** faced the **Syracuse Nationals** in a game that went into **overtime**. With **no foul-out rule limits at the time**, players kept getting disqualified due to excessive fouls.

By the **sixth overtime**, both teams had so few players left that they **couldn't continue playing**, forcing the referees to **declare the game a tie!**

This bizarre event led to new rules preventing teams from ending a game with **too few players to finish!**

Mind-Blowing Basketball Fact #43

MIND-BLOWING BASKETBALL FACT #43

THE NBA PLAYER WHO WAS TRADED... FOR A COPY MACHINE!

NBA trades usually involve players, draft picks, or cash, but one of the strangest trades in history involved... **a copy machine!**

In **1994, the Denver Nuggets** traded **a player named Antonio McDyess** to the **Detroit Pistons** in a multi-team deal. But in a separate move, the **Indiana Pacers** traded **a bench player to the Minnesota Timberwolves in exchange for office equipment—specifically, a brand-new copy machine!**

This remains one of the most **ridiculous trades in NBA history**, proving that sometimes, **teams value office supplies more than players!**

Mind-Blowing Basketball Fact #44

THE NBA PLAYER WHO MADE THE LEAGUE... WITHOUT BEING DRAFTED!

Every NBA player is either **drafted or signed as a free agent**—except for one, who mysteriously appeared on a team without going through either process!

In **1964, Zelmo Beaty** was a dominant college player, but due to a clerical error, his name **was accidentally left off the NBA Draft list.** Despite never being officially selected, the **St. Louis Hawks** still signed him to a contract, making him the only player in NBA history to **bypass both the draft and free agency!**

Beaty went on to have a legendary career, proving that **even a paperwork mistake couldn't stop him from becoming an NBA star!**

Mind-Blowing Basketball Fact #45

MIND-BLOWING BASKETBALL FACT #45

THE NBA GAME THAT WAS DELAYED... BY A GATORADE EXPLOSION!

During a high-stakes matchup in **2007**, chaos erupted not on the court, but in the team's bench area! In the middle of a tense game, a malfunctioning **Gatorade machine** at the arena suddenly burst, spraying the bench, scorers, and even parts of the court with a tidal wave of sports drink.

Officials were forced to halt the game for over **30 minutes** while maintenance crews cleaned up the mess and ensured the electrical systems were safe. This unexpected hydration mishap remains one of the most bizarre delays in NBA history, proving that sometimes even a simple drink can change the game!

Mind-Blowing Basketball Fact #46

MIND-BLOWING BASKETBALL FACT #46

THE NBA PLAYER WHO SCORED 70 POINTS… AND LOST THE GAME!

Scoring **70 points in an NBA game** is an **unbelievable feat**, but imagine dropping that many points… **and still losing!**

On **March 24, 2017, Devin Booker** of the Phoenix Suns put on a **historic performance**, torching the Boston Celtics for **70 points**—becoming the **youngest player ever** to hit that mark. But despite his scoring explosion, the Suns **still lost the game, 130-120.**

To make matters even crazier, Booker's teammates **held up "70" signs and celebrated the milestone,** even though they were getting blown out! The moment sparked controversy, but one thing was clear—**it was one of the most jaw-dropping scoring performances in NBA history.**

Mind-Blowing Basketball Fact #47

MIND-BLOWING BASKETBALL FACT #47

THE NBA GAME THAT WAS DELAYED... BECAUSE OF A STUCK ZAMBONI!

Basketball and hockey often share arenas, but one NBA game was delayed **because a Zamboni got stuck on the court!**

On **March 7, 1997,** the **Boston Celtics** were preparing to play the **Orlando Magic** when arena staff attempted to move a **Zamboni machine off the floor after an earlier hockey game.** Unfortunately, the massive ice-cleaning vehicle **malfunctioned and stalled at center court!**

Players, referees, and fans watched in disbelief as **workers struggled for nearly an hour to remove the Zamboni**, forcing a rare game delay due to **a hockey-related traffic jam.**

A bizarre reminder that sometimes, **basketball and hockey don't mix!**

Mind-Blowing Basketball Fact #48

THE NBA PLAYER WHO WAS FINED... FOR KISSING A REFEREE!

NBA players get fined for many reasons—**fighting, technical fouls, even celebrating too much.** But one player received a fine for something totally unexpected: **kissing a referee!**

During a game in **1999, Dennis Rodman**—known for his wild antics—disagreed with a call but instead of arguing, he **walked up to the ref and planted a kiss on his cheek!** The moment left the official stunned and the crowd laughing, but the NBA wasn't amused. Rodman was **immediately hit with a fine for "inappropriate conduct."**

While the league saw it as unprofessional, it remains one of the **funniest technical fouls in NBA history!**

Mind-Blowing Basketball Fact #49

MIND-BLOWING BASKETBALL FACT #49

THE NBA PLAYER WHO PLAYED FOR THE SAME TEAM... TWICE IN ONE GAME!

Trades and roster moves happen all the time in the NBA, but one player **was traded and then re-signed so fast that he played for the same team twice in a single game!**

On **February 22, 2018,** the **Denver Nuggets** traded **Devin Harris** to the **Dallas Mavericks** during halftime. However, due to a paperwork issue, the trade **was temporarily voided,** forcing Harris to **return to the Nuggets' bench and continue playing in the second half!**

Once the paperwork was sorted, the trade was finalized after the game, making him the only player in NBA history to **play for a team, get traded, and then return to finish the same game.**

# Mind-Blowing Basketball Fact #50

MIND-BLOWING BASKETBALL FACT #50

THE NBA GAME THAT WAS DELAYED... BY A SNAKE IN THE LOCKER ROOM!

NBA teams deal with all kinds of game delays, but one team had to pause their pregame routine... to deal with a snake!

On **March 11, 2016,** the **San Antonio Spurs** were preparing to face the **Sacramento Kings** when players in the visitors' locker room suddenly noticed **a live snake slithering around the floor!** The startled players immediately called for arena staff, who carefully removed the reptile before the game could proceed.

Though no one was injured, the unexpected guest **definitely threw off the pregame routine—** and gave the Spurs a **very unwelcome surprise!**

Mind-Blowing Basketball Fact #51

MIND-BLOWING BASKETBALL FACT #51

THE NBA PLAYER SUSPENDED... FOR BRINGING POPCORN TO PRACTICE

NBA players have been suspended for **fighting, violating league policies, and even missing games**—but one player actually got suspended **for bringing popcorn to practice!**

In **2003, Portland Trail Blazers guard Bonzi Wells** showed up to a team meeting with **a giant tub of popcorn, acting as if it were a movie night.** His coach, **Maurice Cheeks,** was furious at Wells' lack of professionalism and immediately **suspended him for "conduct detrimental to the team."**

It remains one of the strangest reasons for a suspension in NBA history—proving that sometimes, **snacks can cost you your job!**

Mind-Blowing Basketball Fact #52

MIND-BLOWING BASKETBALL FACT #52

THE NBA PLAYER WHO WAS EJECTED... FOR AIR-GUITAR CELEBRATION!

NBA players get ejected for **fighting, arguing with referees, or committing flagrant fouls**—but one player was thrown out of a game for simply **playing air guitar!**

During a **2018 game, Atlanta Hawks guard Taurean Prince** hit a clutch three-pointer and, feeling the energy, celebrated by **pretending to play an air guitar.** The referee, thinking he was taunting the opposing team, **gave him a second technical foul—resulting in an automatic ejection!**

Fans were **stunned** at the bizarre ruling, making it one of the most **ridiculous ejections in NBA history.**

Mind-Blowing Basketball Fact #53

MIND-BLOWING BASKETBALL FACT #53

THE PLAYER WHO WORE TWO DIFFERENT JERSEY NUMBERS IN ONE GAME

Most players stick with **one jersey number** for an entire season, but one NBA star **had to switch numbers in the middle of a game!**

On **February 14, 1990, Michael Jordan's** iconic **#23 jersey went missing** before tip-off in a game against the **Orlando Magic.** With no backup available, Jordan had to **wear a nameless #12 jersey** for the game.

Despite the last-minute uniform change, Jordan still **dropped 49 points**, proving that **it wasn't the jersey number that made him great—it was the man wearing it!**

Mind-Blowing Basketball Fact #54

MIND-BLOWING BASKETBALL FACT #54

THE NBA GAME THAT WAS DELAYED... BECAUSE THE BASKET WAS TOO TALL!

NBA rims are always set at **10 feet high**, but during one game, players noticed something was **way off.**

On **March 6, 2017**, the **Milwaukee Bucks** and **Los Angeles Clippers** were warming up when **Clippers players kept missing shots they normally made.** Upon investigation, officials discovered that **one of the hoops had been set too high—by an extra three inches!**

The game had to be **delayed while workers adjusted the rim** to regulation height. Once fixed, play resumed, but not before players joked that they had been **shooting on a "Shaq-sized" hoop.**

A rare reminder that in the NBA, **even the smallest measurement can change the game!**

Mind-Blowing Basketball Fact #55

MIND-BLOWING BASKETBALL FACT #55

THE NBA PLAYER WHO MISSED A GAME... BECAUSE OF A PEANUT ALLERGY!

Injuries, illnesses, and suspensions are common reasons for missing an NBA game—but one player had to sit out because of **a peanut allergy!**

During the **2009 season, Boston Celtics guard Glen "Big Baby" Davis** was **forced to miss a game** after having an **allergic reaction to peanuts he unknowingly ate.** The reaction was so severe that **team doctors ruled him out** for the night.

While unusual, this incident proves that in the NBA, **sometimes even a snack can sideline a player!**

Mind-Blowing Basketball Fact #56

MIND-BLOWING BASKETBALL FACT #56

THE NBA PLAYER WHO GOT EJECTED... FOR DANCING!

Players usually get ejected for **fighting, arguing with referees, or committing flagrant fouls**—but one player was thrown out **just for dancing!**

During a **2013 game, Milwaukee Bucks center Larry Sanders** celebrated a big play by doing a **quick dance move near the bench.** The referees, believing he was **taunting the opposing team,** hit him with a **second technical foul—resulting in an automatic ejection!**

Sanders was stunned, and fans were left shaking their heads at **one of the most ridiculous ejections in NBA history.**

Mind-Blowing Basketball Fact #57

MIND-BLOWING BASKETBALL FACT #57

THE NBA GAME THAT WAS DELAYED... BECAUSE OF A BROKEN SHOT CLOCK!

NBA games rely on precise timing, but one game was **thrown into chaos** when the **shot clock completely stopped working!**

On **January 14, 2019,** the **Golden State Warriors** and **Denver Nuggets** were set to tip off when **officials realized the shot clock above the backboard was malfunctioning.** Arena staff tried to fix it, but after multiple failed attempts, **they had to bring out a temporary digital clock and place it on the sideline.**

Players had to constantly **glance at the floor** to track the shot clock, making it one of the most **awkwardly played games in recent NBA history!**

Mind-Blowing Basketball Fact #58

MIND-BLOWING BASKETBALL FACT #58

THE PLAYER WHO SIGNED A $30M DEAL... THEN RETIRED THE SAME DAY

Most players dream of signing a massive contract, but one NBA star **secured a $30 million deal—then immediately retired!**

In **2005, Houston Rockets legend Yao Ming** signed a **five-year, $76 million extension**, but due to **persistent foot injuries,** he played only **five games over the next two seasons.** By **2011,** his injuries forced him to **retire from basketball,** leaving millions of dollars on the table.

Despite his short career, Yao **became a global icon,** proving that impact isn't just about longevity—it's about **how much you change the game while you play.**

Mind-Blowing Basketball Fact #59

MIND-BLOWING BASKETBALL FACT #59

THE NBA GAME THAT WAS DELAYED... BECAUSE OF A FREE TACO PROMOTION!

NBA teams love fan giveaways, but one promotion **got so out of hand that it actually delayed a game!**

During a **Los Angeles Lakers home game**, the team was on the verge of scoring **100 points**, which meant fans would **win free tacos** as part of a long-running arena promotion. With seconds left and the Lakers sitting at **99 points**, the crowd began **loudly chanting "WE WANT TACOS!"**

The players, caught up in the moment, **started forcing wild shots just to hit 100.** When they finally did, the **crowd erupted so loudly that play had to be paused** before the game could finish!

A legendary moment that proved sometimes, **fans care about free food just as much as basketball!**

Mind-Blowing Basketball Fact #60

MIND-BLOWING BASKETBALL FACT #60

THE NBA PLAYER WHO ONCE SCORED 0 POINTS... BUT STILL WON FINALS MVP!

Scoring is usually the key to winning **NBA Finals MVP**, but one player **won the award despite recording a game with 0 points!**

In **1978, Wes Unseld** led the **Washington Bullets** to their first-ever NBA Championship. Known for his **dominant rebounding and defense,** Unseld didn't rely on scoring—he focused on **controlling the game in other ways.**

Despite averaging just **9 points per game in the Finals,** he won **Finals MVP,** becoming one of the **few players ever to win the award without being a top scorer.**

A reminder that in basketball, **impact isn't always measured by points!**

Mind-Blowing Basketball Fact #61

MIND-BLOWING BASKETBALL FACT #61

THE NBA GAME THAT WAS DELAYED... BECAUSE OF A MISSING REFEREE!

NBA games can't start without referees, but one game was **delayed because an official simply didn't show up!**

On **December 1, 2017,** the **Miami Heat** and **New York Knicks** were ready for tip-off when players and coaches realized something was **off— only two referees were on the court instead of three!**

After scrambling for answers, league officials discovered that the **third referee was stuck in traffic and couldn't make it on time!** The game was **delayed for nearly 20 minutes** before the NBA decided to play with just two refs until the missing official arrived in the second quarter.

A rare reminder that sometimes, **even referees need load management!**

Mind-Blowing Basketball Fact #62

MIND-BLOWING BASKETBALL FACT #62

THE NBA PLAYER WHO WAS DRAFTED... BUT DIDN'T EXIST!

NBA teams spend months scouting players, but in **1977**, one team **accidentally drafted a completely fictional player!**

The **Milwaukee Bucks** front office staff decided to play a prank and submitted the name **"John Smith" from "Sensebaugh State"** as their late-round pick. The problem? **Neither the player nor the school existed!**

The NBA quickly caught the joke and **voided the selection,** but for a brief moment, the Bucks had drafted someone who **wasn't real!**

One of the most bizarre draft moments in history — and proof that even NBA teams have a sense of humor!

Mind-Blowing Basketball Fact #63

MIND-BLOWING BASKETBALL FACT #63

THE NBA PLAYER WHO GOT A TECHNICAL FOUL... FOR HIGH-FIVING A REFEREE!

NBA players get technical fouls for **arguing, taunting, or unsportsmanlike conduct**—but one player was hit with a **tech just for high-fiving a referee!**

During a **2016 game, Kris Dunn** of the **Minnesota Timberwolves** made a great defensive play, and in the excitement, he instinctively **high-fived the referee** standing nearby. The ref, caught off guard, called **a technical foul for "excessive contact" with an official!**

The crowd **burst into laughter**, but the call stood—making it one of the **strangest technical fouls in NBA history!**

Mind-Blowing Basketball Fact #64

MIND-BLOWING BASKETBALL FACT #64

THE NBA PLAYER WHO LOST A SHOE... AND KEPT PLAYING!

Most players need **both shoes** to play at the highest level, but one NBA star **kept playing—even after losing one mid-game!**

During a **2014 game, Golden State Warriors guard Stephen Curry** had his sneaker **fly off while making a move.** Instead of stopping play, Curry **continued dribbling, hit a pass, and even played defense—wearing just one shoe!**

Fans were **stunned** as he **dodged defenders barefoot** before finally getting a break to put his shoe back on.

It was a hilarious moment that proved **nothing—not even missing a shoe—can slow down a superstar!**

Mind-Blowing Basketball Fact #65

THE PLAYER WHO WORE GOGGLES AFTER A BRUTAL EYE INJURY

Some NBA players wear goggles for medical reasons, but one legend **started wearing them** after getting poked in the eye by an opponent—twice!

In **1980, Kareem Abdul-Jabbar**, already one of the most dominant players in NBA history, suffered **two serious eye injuries** from accidental (and not-so-accidental) pokes. To protect himself, he **began wearing signature goggles** for the rest of his career.

His new look became so iconic that today, **goggles are practically synonymous with Kareem!**

Mind-Blowing Basketball Fact #66

MIND-BLOWING BASKETBALL FACT #66

THE NBA GAME THAT WAS DELAYED... BECAUSE OF A FIRE ALARM!

NBA games get delayed for all sorts of reasons, but one game was **brought to a sudden halt... because of a fire alarm!**

On **March 12, 2018,** the **Toronto Raptors** were playing the **Indiana Pacers** when a **fire alarm suddenly went off in the arena.** Players, coaches, and fans were forced to **evacuate the building** while firefighters investigated the cause.

After a long delay, officials discovered **there was no actual fire—just a malfunction in the system!** The game eventually resumed, but not before everyone got a **surprise fire drill they never expected!**

Mind-Blowing Basketball Fact #67

MIND-BLOWING BASKETBALL FACT #67

THE NBA PLAYER WHO ONCE GOT A TRIPLE-DOUBLE... WITHOUT POINTS!

Triple-doubles usually involve **points, rebounds, and assists**, but one NBA player achieved the rarest kind—without scoring a single point!

On **February 3, 2017, Draymond Green** of the **Golden State Warriors** recorded a **triple-double with 12 rebounds, 10 assists, and 10 steals**—but scored only 4 points!

Even crazier, he could have had a **quadruple-double**, as he also had **5 blocks** in the game.

It remains the **only triple-double in NBA history that didn't include double-digit points!** A true testament to **defense and playmaking over scoring!**

Mind-Blowing Basketball Fact #68

MIND-BLOWING BASKETBALL FACT #68

THE NBA PLAYER WHO PLAYED IN 5 DIFFERENT DECADES!

Most NBA careers last **a decade or two**, but one player defied time by playing in **five different decades!**

Vince Carter, known for his **legendary dunks and clutch performances,** became the **first and only player in NBA history** to play in the **1990s, 2000s, 2010s, and even the 2020s** before retiring in 2020.

His career spanned an incredible **22 seasons**, proving that **age is just a number when you love the game!**

Mind-Blowing Basketball Fact #69

MIND-BLOWING BASKETBALL FACT #69

THE NBA GAME THAT WAS DELAYED... BECAUSE OF A MISSING NET!

NBA hoops are **carefully inspected before every game,** but one night, the game couldn't start because the **basket was missing a net!**

On **March 20, 2013,** the **Los Angeles Lakers** were warming up for their game when players noticed **one of the baskets had no net attached.** Officials scrambled to find a replacement, but arena staff **couldn't locate a spare net right away,** forcing an unexpected delay.

After several awkward minutes, they finally installed a net, and the game tipped off—proving that sometimes, **it's the smallest details that can stop the game!**

Mind-Blowing Basketball Fact #70

MIND-BLOWING BASKETBALL FACT #70

THE NBA PLAYER WHO PICKED FAST FOOD OVER BASKETBALL

Most players dream of being drafted into the NBA, but one player **walked away from basketball—to work at McDonald's!**

In **1977,** the **New Orleans Jazz** selected **Lusia Harris**, making her the **first and only woman officially drafted by an NBA team.** However, she declined the opportunity, citing that the **NBA was a men's league** and instead chose to work **a regular job at McDonald's** before eventually becoming a basketball coach.

Despite never playing in the league, Harris is recognized as a **trailblazer in basketball history**, proving that sometimes, **legacy is bigger than the game itself.**

Mind-Blowing Basketball Fact #71

MIND-BLOWING BASKETBALL FACT #71

THE NBA PLAYER WHO SCORED 13 POINTS IN 33 SECONDS!

Most teams struggle to score **13 points in a quarter**, but one player did it in just **33 seconds!**

On **December 9, 2004**, **Tracy McGrady** pulled off one of the greatest comebacks in NBA history. With his **Houston Rockets** trailing the **San Antonio Spurs** in the final minute, McGrady went on an **unstoppable scoring spree—hitting four three-pointers and a free throw in just 33 seconds!**

His final shot, a **contested three with 1.7 seconds left,** won the game, leaving fans and players **completely speechless.**

It remains one of the most **unbelievable clutch performances ever witnessed in the NBA!**

100 MIND-BLOWING BASKETBALL FACTS

Mind-Blowing Basketball Fact #72

MIND-BLOWING BASKETBALL FACT #72

THE NBA GAME THAT WAS PLAYED IN TOTAL SILENCE!

NBA arenas are known for **loud crowds and booming sound systems**, but one game was played in **complete silence!**

On **April 17, 2015,** the **Golden State Warriors** and the **New Orleans Pelicans** played a preseason game in an empty arena—**with no fans, no music, and no announcers.** This eerie environment was due to the **COVID-19 pandemic restrictions**, forcing teams to **compete in an empty gym.**

Players later described it as **one of the strangest games ever**, saying it felt more like a **high-stakes practice than an actual NBA matchup!**

A true reminder of how much **fans bring the game to life!**

Mind-Blowing Basketball Fact #73

MIND-BLOWING BASKETBALL FACT #73

THE NBA PLAYER WHO ONCE SCORED 100 POINTS... IN JUST 20 MINUTES!

Scoring **100 points in a game** is legendary, but imagine doing it **in just one half!**

In **1978, college basketball player Clarence "Bevo" Francis** put on one of the most **unbelievable scoring performances in history.** Playing for **Rio Grande College,** he **dropped 100 points in just 20 minutes** before being subbed out for the entire second half!

While this didn't happen in the NBA, it remains one of the **fastest 100-point performances ever recorded**—a feat so absurd that it's hard to believe!

A true example of what happens when a player **gets hotter than anyone thought possible!**

Mind-Blowing Basketball Fact #74

MIND-BLOWING BASKETBALL FACT #74

THE NBA PLAYER WHO WAS EJECTED... FOR YAWNING!

NBA referees eject players for **fighting, technical fouls, or unsportsmanlike conduct**—but one player was **thrown out just for yawning!**

During a **2012 game, Metta World Peace (formerly Ron Artest)** was hit with a **technical foul for arguing with a referee.** As he walked away, he let out an exaggerated **yawn**, clearly mocking the official. The referee **took offense and immediately gave him a second technical foul—resulting in an automatic ejection!**

Fans were stunned, making this one of the most **ridiculous ejections in NBA history!**

A reminder that in the NBA, **even yawning at the wrong time can get you kicked out!**

Mind-Blowing Basketball Fact #75

MIND-BLOWING BASKETBALL FACT #75

THE NBA GAME THAT WAS DELAYED... BECAUSE OF A LEAKING ROOF!

Basketball is played indoors to **avoid bad weather**, but one NBA game was **stopped mid-play** because of **rain leaking through the roof!**

On **January 26, 2018,** the **New Orleans Pelicans** were facing the **Indiana Pacers** when referees noticed **water dripping onto the court** from a leak in the Smoothie King Center's roof. Players had to be **sent to the locker room** while arena staff frantically tried to stop the leak.

After a **two-hour delay**, the game was finally called off—making it one of the few NBA games ever canceled because of **bad weather... inside the arena!**

Mind-Blowing Basketball Fact #76

MIND-BLOWING BASKETBALL FACT #76

THE NBA PLAYER WHO SIGNED A CONTRACT... THAT PAID HIM FOR 30 YEARS!

Most NBA contracts pay players over a few seasons, but **one player negotiated a deal that paid him for 30 years—long after he retired!**

In **2000,** the **New York Knicks** signed **Allan Houston** to a massive contract, but it wasn't the most famous long-term deal in NBA history. That honor belongs to **Bonzi Wells**, who structured his deal in a way that **paid him small annual installments for 30 years instead of receiving it all upfront.**

This kind of contract, often called a **deferred payment deal,** is similar to what **MLB's Bobby Bonilla** did, ensuring he still gets paid **decades after his playing days ended.**

A genius financial move that proves **smart contracts can outlast your career!**

Mind-Blowing Basketball Fact #77

MIND-BLOWING BASKETBALL FACT #77

THE NBA GAME THAT WAS DELAYED... BECAUSE OF TOO MUCH POPCORN!

NBA arenas are designed to **handle big crowds**, but one game was delayed because of **a popcorn disaster!**

During a **2014 game**, the **Sacramento Kings** locker room was accidentally **flooded with popcorn** after a mischievous arena worker **spilled an entire industrial-sized bag inside.** The mess was so massive that **players couldn't enter the locker room**, forcing a delay while the team scrambled to clean up.

The incident became a legendary prank, but it also proved that in the NBA, **even popcorn can cause chaos!**

Mind-Blowing Basketball Fact #78

MIND-BLOWING BASKETBALL FACT #78

THE NBA PLAYER WHO PLAYED A GAME WEARING A HOSPITAL WRISTBAND

Most players **rest after a hospital visit,** but one **NBA star went straight from the hospital to the court—without even removing his wristband!**

On **May 7, 2015, Chicago Bulls star Taj Gibson** was dealing with a stomach illness so severe that he was **hospitalized earlier that day.** But just hours later, Gibson **checked himself out, arrived at the arena, and suited up for a playoff game against the Cleveland Cavaliers.**

Fans noticed he was still **wearing his hospital wristband** during warmups, making it clear that he had **literally just been discharged!**

A true example of **commitment and toughness in the NBA!**

Mind-Blowing Basketball Fact #79

MIND-BLOWING BASKETBALL FACT #79

THE NBA PLAYER WHO WAS TRADED... FOR A WASHING MACHINE!

NBA players are usually traded for **other players, draft picks, or cash**, but one player was **literally traded for a washing machine!**

In **1964,** the **St. Louis Hawks** traded **big man Bill Spivey** to the **Baltimore Bullets.** But instead of receiving a player or money in return, the Hawks **asked for a brand-new washing machine** to be used in their locker room!

This remains one of the **strangest trades in NBA history**, proving that sometimes, **teams prioritize clean jerseys over new talent!**

Mind-Blowing Basketball Fact #80

MIND-BLOWING BASKETBALL FACT #80

THE NBA PLAYER WHO ONCE BLOCKED 17 SHOTS IN A SINGLE GAME!

Blocking shots is one of the most dominant defensive plays in basketball, but one player **took it to an entirely different level—swatting away 17 shots in one game!**

On **October 28, 1973, Elmore Smith** of the **Los Angeles Lakers** set the **NBA record for most blocks in a single game** with **17 rejections** against the Portland Trail Blazers.

To put that in perspective, some teams don't even record **17 blocks in an entire week!** Smith's shot-blocking masterpiece still stands as one of the most **untouchable records in NBA history.**

Mind-Blowing Basketball Fact #81

MIND-BLOWING BASKETBALL FACT #81

THE NBA GAME THAT WAS DELAYED... BECAUSE OF A BROKEN BACKBOARD!

Dunking is one of the most exciting plays in basketball, but sometimes, **it's too powerful for the equipment to handle!**

On **April 23, 1993, Shaquille O'Neal** delivered a **thunderous dunk** against the **New Jersey Nets** that not only shattered the backboard—but **completely tore down the entire hoop structure!**

The game had to be **delayed for nearly an hour** while arena staff scrambled to **install a brand-new hoop.** This led the NBA to **reinforce all backboards and rims** to prevent future backboard-smashing chaos.

A true reminder that when Shaq dunks, **even the basket isn't safe!**

Mind-Blowing Basketball Fact #82

MIND-BLOWING BASKETBALL FACT #82

THE NBA PLAYER WHO ONCE RECORDED A "DOUBLE TRIPLE-DOUBLE"!

A **triple-double** is impressive, but one player took it **to the next level** by recording **a double triple-double!**

On **March 18, 1968, Wilt Chamberlain** put up an **unbelievable stat line** of **22 points, 25 rebounds, and 21 assists**—becoming the first and only player in NBA history to record **at least 20 in three different statistical categories.**

This "double triple-double" remains **one of the rarest feats in basketball history**, proving once again that **Wilt's records might never be broken!**

Mind-Blowing Basketball Fact #83

MIND-BLOWING BASKETBALL FACT #83

THE NBA GAME THAT WAS PLAYED ON A COURT WITH NO THREE-POINT LINE!

The **three-point line** has been a game-changer in modern basketball, but one bizarre NBA game was played **without it—by accident!**

On **October 13, 1979,** the **Boston Celtics** hosted the **Philadelphia 76ers** in a preseason game, but when players arrived, they noticed something strange—the **arena's court was missing the three-point arc!**

Due to an **installation error,** the floor crew forgot to paint the line, forcing the teams to **play the entire game as if the three-pointer didn't exist.**

It was a strange throwback to the pre-three-point era, proving that **even the smallest detail can change how the game is played!**

Mind-Blowing Basketball Fact #84

MIND-BLOWING BASKETBALL FACT #84

THE NBA PLAYER WHO WORE THE WRONG SHORTS... FOR AN ENTIRE GAME!

NBA players have **carefully planned uniforms**, but one player unknowingly **wore the wrong shorts for an entire game!**

During a **1999 game, San Antonio Spurs forward Tim Duncan** suited up as usual—except there was one problem: **he was wearing his warm-up practice shorts instead of his official game shorts!**

Duncan didn't even realize it until **the second half**, but since the uniform violation wasn't major, referees **let him continue playing.**

The incident became a **funny footnote** in his legendary career, proving that even **future Hall of Famers can forget their game-day gear!**

Mind-Blowing Basketball Fact #85

MIND-BLOWING BASKETBALL FACT #85

THE NBA PLAYER WHO WAS FINED... FOR WEARING TOO MANY HEADBANDS!

Headbands are a common accessory in the NBA, but one player was actually **fined for wearing too many at once!**

In **2005, Boston Celtics guard Paul Pierce** decided to make a fashion statement by **wearing two headbands stacked on top of each other** during a game. However, the NBA had a strict rule that **players could only wear one headband at a time.**

The league quickly issued a **fine for violating uniform policy,** forcing Pierce to **retire his double-headband look forever.**

A hilarious moment that proved even in the NBA, **fashion choices come with rules!**

Mind-Blowing Basketball Fact #86

MIND-BLOWING BASKETBALL FACT #86

THE NBA PLAYER WHO SCORED A BASKET... WHILE LYING ON THE FLOOR!

Scoring in the NBA usually requires **jumping, cutting, or sprinting**, but one player **managed to score while lying flat on his back!**

During a **2006 game**, **Steve Nash** of the **Phoenix Suns** drove to the basket, got fouled, and fell hard to the floor. But instead of giving up on the play, Nash **threw the ball up from his back— AND MADE THE SHOT!**

The crowd erupted as Nash casually got up like it was just another bucket, proving that in basketball, **you don't always need to be standing to score!**

Mind-Blowing Basketball Fact #87

MIND-BLOWING BASKETBALL FACT #87

THE NBA GAME DELAYED BY A BROKEN SHOT CLOCK

Shot clocks are essential in basketball, but one game was **delayed for nearly an hour** because the **arena didn't have a backup!**

On **January 20, 2019,** the **Houston Rockets** were set to play the **Washington Wizards** when the **shot clock above the backboard suddenly stopped working.** Normally, arenas have a **backup shot clock** ready, but this time, there was **none available!**

As a last-minute solution, the NBA placed a **temporary digital clock on the sidelines**, forcing players to **constantly look away from the basket** to track the time.

It made for one of the most awkward games ever, proving that even **high-tech NBA arenas aren't always prepared for the unexpected!**

Mind-Blowing Basketball Fact #88

MIND-BLOWING BASKETBALL FACT #88

THE PLAYER WHO SCORED 50 POINTS... WITHOUT A SINGLE THREE

In today's NBA, most **high-scoring performances** are fueled by three-pointers, but one player dropped 50 points—without making a single shot from deep!

On **December 29, 2018, LaMarcus Aldridge** of the **San Antonio Spurs** exploded for **56 points against the Oklahoma City Thunder**. The most shocking part? He **didn't attempt a single three-pointer!**

Instead, Aldridge dominated with **mid-range jumpers and post moves**, proving that even in the modern game, **old-school scoring can still get the job done!**

Mind-Blowing Basketball Fact #89

MIND-BLOWING BASKETBALL FACT #89

THE NBA PLAYER WHO WORE THREE DIFFERENT JERSEYS IN ONE GAME!

Most NBA players wear the **same jersey for an entire game**, but one player had to **change his uniform three times in a single night!**

On **March 9, 2021, New Orleans Pelicans star Zion Williamson** had such an **explosive performance** that he **ripped two of his jerseys** during the game against the **Memphis Grizzlies**.

Each time, he had to **swap jerseys mid-game**, making him the first player in recent history to **wear three different jerseys in one night!**

A hilarious reminder that sometimes, **sheer power comes at the cost of your own uniform!**

Mind-Blowing Basketball Fact #90

MIND-BLOWING BASKETBALL FACT #90

THE PLAYER WHO SIGNED A CONTRACT... THEN RETIRED THE SAME DAY

Signing an NBA contract is usually the start of a new chapter, but one player **signed a deal and retired on the exact same day!**

On **August 1, 2012, Jameson Curry** signed a **10-day contract with the Los Angeles Clippers.** However, before he even got a chance to play, he **announced his retirement just hours later!**

Curry became the **only player in NBA history to retire on the same day he signed his contract**, making his career one of the shortest—if not the shortest—of all time.

A wild moment that proves in the NBA, **some careers end before they even begin!**

Mind-Blowing Basketball Fact #91

MIND-BLOWING BASKETBALL FACT #91

THE NBA GAME THAT WAS DELAYED... BECAUSE THE LIGHTS WENT OUT!

NBA arenas are equipped with **state-of-the-art lighting**, but one game was suddenly **plunged into darkness!**

On **January 5, 2013,** during a game between the **Miami Heat** and the **Atlanta Hawks**, the **arena lights unexpectedly went out mid-play,** causing complete chaos on the court. Players and fans were left **standing in the dark** as officials scrambled to fix the issue.

After a **15-minute delay,** the lights finally came back on, and play resumed—but the bizarre blackout remains one of the strangest **in-game power failures** in NBA history!

Mind-Blowing Basketball Fact #92

MIND-BLOWING BASKETBALL FACT #92

THE NBA PLAYER WHO SCORED 0 POINTS... BUT STILL HAD A PERFECT GAME!

Scoring is a huge part of basketball, but one player **had a perfect game—without scoring a single point!**

On **February 15, 2019, Draymond Green** of the **Golden State Warriors** finished a game with **0 points, 12 rebounds, 11 assists, and 5 steals.** Despite not scoring, he was still the most impactful player on the court, leading his team to victory.

Green became the **first player in NBA history to record a double-double without making a field goal or free throw**, proving that **greatness isn't always about putting the ball in the basket!**

Mind-Blowing Basketball Fact #93

MIND-BLOWING BASKETBALL FACT #93

THE NBA GAME DELAYED BY A PLAYER HANGING ON THE RIM

NBA players love **throwing down monster dunks**, but one dunk caused such a delay that **it nearly stopped the game!**

During a **1993 game, Shaquille O'Neal** delivered a **thunderous dunk**, but instead of letting go, he **hung on the rim for too long**—causing the entire hoop structure to bend and nearly collapse.

The game was **paused for nearly 30 minutes** as the arena crew had to **reassemble and reinforce the basket** before play could continue.

Shaq's dunking power was so legendary that the NBA had to **redesign its entire backboard system** to prevent future rim-rattling disasters!

Mind-Blowing Basketball Fact #94

MIND-BLOWING BASKETBALL FACT #94

THE PLAYER WHO BLOCKED MORE SHOTS THAN AN ENTIRE TEAM

Shot-blocking is a valuable skill, but one player was so dominant that **he single-handedly out-blocked an entire team!**

On **February 18, 1985, Manute Bol**, the 7'7" shot-blocking machine for the **Washington Bullets**, recorded **15 blocks in a single game** against the **Atlanta Hawks**. In comparison, the entire Hawks team **only had 6 blocks combined!**

Bol's defensive masterpiece remains one of the most lopsided shot-blocking performances in NBA history, proving that **sometimes, one player can shut down an entire offense!**

Mind-Blowing Basketball Fact #95

MIND-BLOWING BASKETBALL FACT #95

THE NBA PLAYER WHO GOT EJECTED... BEFORE THE GAME EVEN STARTED!

Getting ejected from a game is rare, but one NBA player **was thrown out before the opening tip-off!**

On **December 3, 2019, New York Knicks forward Marcus Morris** got into a **heated argument with referees during warm-ups**—before the game had even begun. The officials didn't appreciate his attitude, and in a stunning decision, **they ejected him before he could step on the court for a single second of play!**

This made him one of the **only players in NBA history to be disqualified before the game even officially started**—a record that's as bizarre as it is unforgettable!

Mind-Blowing Basketball Fact #96

MIND-BLOWING BASKETBALL FACT #96

THE NBA GAME THAT WAS DELAYED... BECAUSE A BAT INVADED THE COURT!

NBA games have been interrupted for all kinds of reasons, but one was **delayed because of an unexpected flying intruder—a live bat!**

On **October 31, 2009** (fittingly, Halloween night), a game between the **San Antonio Spurs** and the **Sacramento Kings** came to a sudden halt when a **bat swooped down into the arena**, circling the court and disrupting play.

As security scrambled to remove it, **Spurs legend Manu Ginóbili took matters into his own hands—literally.** He **swatted the bat out of midair with his bare hand**, stunning the crowd and instantly becoming a viral sensation.

The bat was safely removed, and Ginóbili walked away as the only NBA player with **both a championship ring and a bat-hunting highlight!**

Mind-Blowing Basketball Fact #97

MIND-BLOWING BASKETBALL FACT #97

THE NBA PLAYER WHO ONCE PLAYED FOR TWO TEAMS... IN THE SAME GAME!

Trades happen all the time in the NBA, but one player **actually played for two different teams in the same game!**

On **November 17, 1978, Eric Money** started the game playing for the **New Jersey Nets** against the **Philadelphia 76ers**. However, due to a controversial officiating error, the NBA ordered **part of the game to be replayed at a later date.**

By the time the game resumed, Money had been **traded to the 76ers**, meaning he **finished the game playing for the opposing team!**

This bizarre sequence made him the **only player in NBA history to play for two teams in the same official game!**

Mind-Blowing Basketball Fact #98

MIND-BLOWING BASKETBALL FACT #98

THE ONLY FINALS MVP WHO NEVER STARTED A GAME

Winning **NBA Finals MVP** is one of the greatest honors in basketball, but one player made history by winning it **without ever starting a game!**

In **2015, Andre Iguodala** of the **Golden State Warriors** came off the bench for most of the season, but when the **NBA Finals** arrived, everything changed. Midway through the series, coach **Steve Kerr inserted him into the starting lineup** to slow down LeBron James. The move worked—**Iguodala played lockdown defense and hit clutch shots**, helping the Warriors win the title.

Despite not being a regular starter, Iguodala was named **Finals MVP**, becoming the **first and only player in NBA history to win the award without starting every game of the series!**

Mind-Blowing Basketball Fact #99

MIND-BLOWING BASKETBALL FACT #99

THE NBA PLAYER WHO WAS DRAFTED... BUT NEVER PLAYED A SINGLE GAME!

Getting drafted into the NBA is a dream for most players, but one player was selected #1 overall—yet never played a single game!

In **1951, the Baltimore Bullets** selected **Gene Melchiorre** with the **first overall pick** in the NBA Draft. However, before he could step onto an NBA court, he was **banned for life** due to his involvement in a **college point-shaving scandal.**

As a result, Melchiorre holds the unique and unfortunate record as **the only #1 draft pick in NBA history to never play a single game!**

Mind-Blowing Basketball Fact #100

MIND-BLOWING BASKETBALL FACT #100

THE NBA PLAYER WHO SCORED 100 POINTS... BUT THERE'S NO VIDEO PROOF!

Wilt Chamberlain's legendary **100-point game** on **March 2, 1962,** is one of the greatest achievements in sports history—but incredibly, **no full video footage exists!**

At the time, NBA games weren't regularly televised, and there were **no cameras recording the game.** The only proof of Chamberlain's performance comes from **radio broadcasts, newspaper reports, and the famous photo of him holding a sheet of paper with "100" written on it.**

Despite the lack of video evidence, his record still stands today—making it the most **iconic unseen moment in basketball history!**

CONCLUSION

Congratulations! You've just experienced *100 Mind-Blowing Basketball Facts*—a journey through the **wildest, most unexpected, and jaw-dropping moments in hoops history.** From legendary performances to bizarre rule changes, from record-breaking feats to absolute chaos on the court, this book has proven one thing: **basketball is anything but predictable.**

But here's the beauty of the game—it's **always evolving.** For every fact you've read, there are **countless more stories waiting to unfold.** Maybe this book has deepened your appreciation for basketball, introduced you to moments you never knew existed, or even inspired you to **dig into the sport's rich and unpredictable history.**

The truth is, the world of basketball is **full of surprises.** You don't need to be in an arena to witness greatness—you just need **curiosity, passion, and a love for the game.**

So, as you close this book, don't think of it as the final buzzer. **Think of it as halftime—because the next mind-blowing moment in basketball is always just around the corner.**

Until next time, stay curious, stay passionate, and remember: **the greatest moments in basketball are the ones we never see coming.**

ACKNOWLEDGEMENTS

Creating *100 Mind-Blowing Basketball Facts* has been an absolute slam dunk of a journey—one filled with passion, persistence, and plenty of buzzer-beater moments. While my name may be on the cover, this book wouldn't have come to life without the inspiration, support, and contributions of some truly amazing people.

First, a massive thank you to **basketball fans, historians, and trivia lovers** who have kept the game's wildest stories alive. Your passion for hoops and the unbelievable moments that shape the sport have been a constant source of inspiration. This book is a celebration of those unforgettable stories.

To my **family and friends**, who patiently listened to me ramble about record-breaking performances, bizarre rule changes, and the quirkiest moments in basketball history—you're the real MVPs. Your support and enthusiasm fueled this project from start to finish.

A special shoutout to my **readers**—whether you picked up this book to relive basketball's craziest moments, to dominate trivia night, or just to experience the pure unpredictability of the game, this book is for you. Your curiosity and love for basketball are what keep these stories alive and thriving.

And finally, to the game of basketball itself — **thank you for being as electrifying, unpredictable, and inspiring as ever.** The stories in this book are just a glimpse into the magic of the game, and I can't wait to see what history-defying moments basketball gives us next.

Here's to hoops, to the legends, and to the moments that leave us speechless.

ABOUT THE AUTHOR

Felix Grayson is a storyteller at heart, driven by an insatiable curiosity for the **strange, surprising, and downright unpredictable moments in sports.** With a passion for uncovering the wildest and most unbelievable tales from the world of basketball, Felix has crafted *100 Mind-Blowing Basketball Facts* to entertain, amaze, and spark wonder in fans of all ages.

When he's not digging through archives or chasing down the next quirky hoops moment, Felix enjoys **shooting around at local courts, diving into classic basketball documentaries, and debating the greatest players of all time over a courtside snack.** A firm believer in the magic of the game and the power of a good story, Felix invites you to take this journey through basketball's most jaw-dropping moments, proving that the sport is just as full of surprises off the court as it is on.

www.ingramcontent.com/pod-product-compliance
Lightning Source LLC
Chambersburg PA
CBHW030318080526
44584CB00012B/613